Dear Moon

Dear Moon

Inspiration from the Beautiful Wisdom of the Qur'an

Zayneb Haleem

Andrews McMeel
PUBLISHING®

Assalamu Alaikum and peace be upon you, dear readers.

My name is Zayneb Haleem and I am honored to welcome you to this book; a heartfelt collection of illustrations inspired by some of my favorite Qur'anic and Islamic verses combined with my own reflections and words. This book is more than just an artistic endeavor. It is a piece of my soul, a journey through faith, the inspiring words of the Qur'an, and my own thoughts in an art form.

Growing up in a home where the beauty of the Qur'an was constantly present, I found myself captivated by the words of Allah and the deep wisdom they convey. As a child, I went to the local mosque with my siblings every day after school, where we learned to recite and understand the basics of the Qur'an. As I grew older, my desire to learn more about the Qur'an and Islam deepened, leading me to pursue further Islamic education to explore the Qur'an's profound meanings and other teachings of Islam.

Alongside this, I've also always been passionate about art. Ever since childhood, I've been captivated by anything creative. I remember my school notebooks often ended with two pages full of doodles, and my mom used to give me pattern books or cookbooks instead of toys, knowing I preferred looking at the pictures and colors. As I grew up, I also loved designing my own clothes, combining patterns and color combinations with my mom's help, and we spent countless hours drawing and sketching together. This fascination with the visual still helps me when finding inspiration for my illustrations today.

Over the years, I learned that I've always found it easier to communicate and express my emotions through illustrations rather than words. As my passion for illustrating grew and I began sharing my work, I discovered that my artwork resonated with others, offering them a new perspective and a sense of peace and reflection.

In this book, you will find illustrations of my favorite Qur'anic and Islamic verses. Alongside these passages, I have included some of my own words—reflections, thoughts, and insights— that emerged during my life and the process of creating this book. My intention is to provide you with a space for reflection; a moment to pause and connect with the divine message, and an opportunity to find inspiration in your daily life.

This book is an invitation to reflect on the verses and their relevance in your life. Whether you choose to read this book from cover to cover or dip in and out as the mood strikes you, the messages within are timeless, and each visit to these pages can offer valuable insights into any situation in life.

It is my hope that this book will be a source of comfort, inspiration, and joy for readers of all ages. I hope it will make you feel motivated and hopeful. Art has a unique way of speaking to the heart, and it is my sincere wish this book will touch your soul, inspire your faith, and guide you toward the right path.

Zayneb

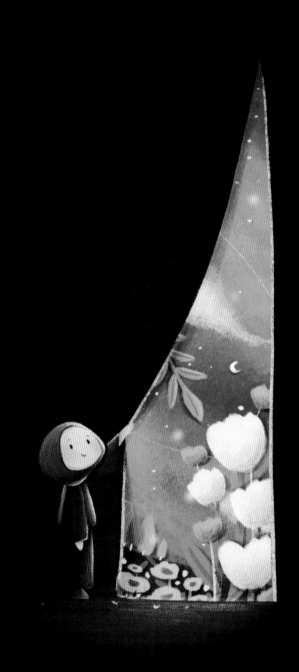

BETTER DAYS
ARE COMING
INSHALLAH

HE HAS
MADE ME
BLESSED WHEREVER
I AM...
QUR'AN 19:31

Nothing Will
ever befall us
Except what Allah
has destined for us

QUR'AN 9:51

OH ALLAH, FIx MY HEARt

HAVE FAITH IN THE BEAUTY
OF ALLAH'S PLAN

AND LET PATIENCE
LIGHT YOUR PATH...

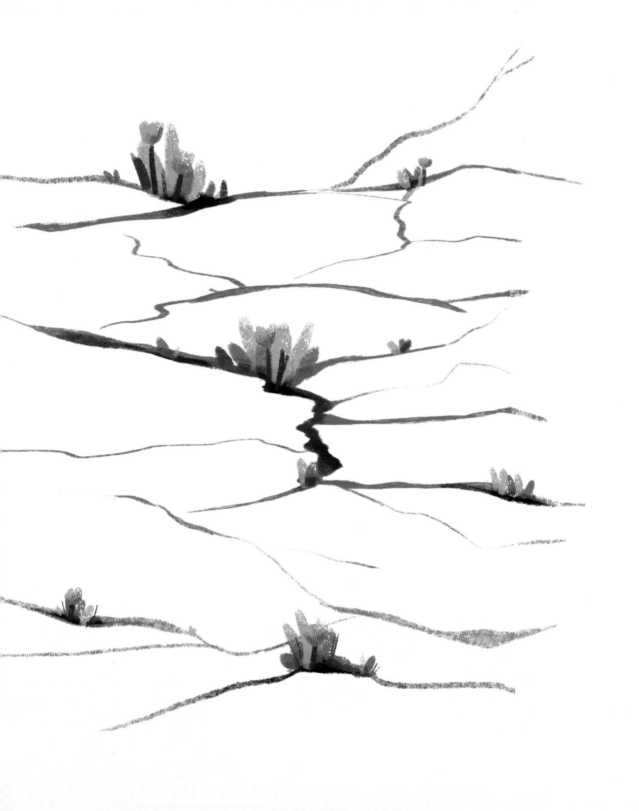

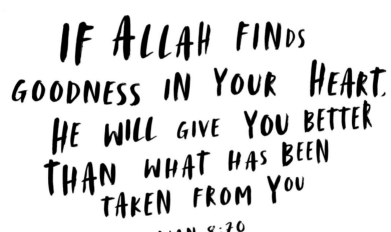

IF ALLAH FINDS GOODNESS IN YOUR HEART, HE WILL GIVE YOU BETTER THAN WHAT HAS BEEN TAKEN FROM YOU

QUR'AN 8:70

MY LORD
PUT MY HEART
AT PEACE FOR ME

JUST AS ALLAH TURNS
NIGHT INTO DAY,

HE CAN UNDOUBTEDLY TRANSFORM YOUR SORROWS INTO BLISS AND SUCCESS...

Guide us
to the
STRAIGHT
path

QUR'AN 1:6

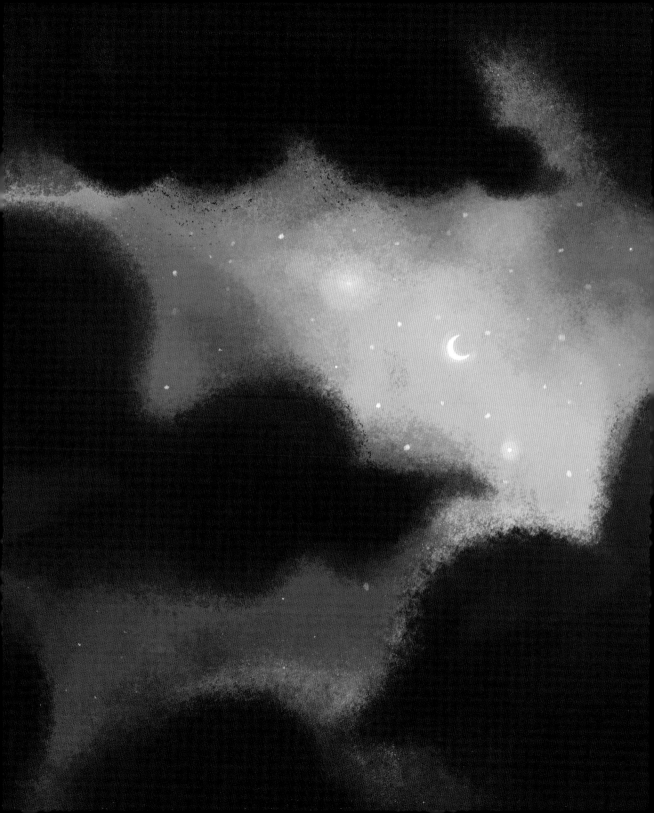

CALL UPON ME; I WILL RESPOND TO YOU

QUR'AN 40:60

SOMETIMES, TALKING TO
ALLAH IS ALL YOU NEED...

IF YOU ARE GRATEFUL, I WILL CERTAINLY GIVE YOU MORE

QUR'AN 14:7

THEN WHICH OF YOUR LORD'S

FAVORS WILL YOU DENY?

QUR'AN 55:13

ALLAH KNows...
HE KNOWS IT ALL

WHOEVER BELIEVES
IN ALLAH,
HE WILL GUIDE HIS HEART

QUR'AN 64:11

WHO ELSE CAN BETTER
UNDERSTAND
YOUR HEART THAN THE
ONE WHO CREATED IT...

DO NOT LET THEIR
WORDS SADDEN YOU

QUR'AN 10:65

ALLAH
KNOWS YOUR
SILENT
PRAYERS...

INDEED
I AM NEAR
QUR'AN 2:186

LIGHT UPON LIGHT.
ALLAH GUIDES TO
HIS LIGHT WHOM
HE WILLS

QUR'AN 24:35

HE FOUND YOU LOST
AND GUIDED YOU

QUR'AN 93:1

WHAT's
YOURS
WILL
FIND
YOU...

ALLAH
DOES NOT BURDEN
ANY SOUL
WITH MORE THAN
IT CAN BEAR

QUR'AN 2:286

So REMEMBER ME—
I WILL REMEMBER YOU

QUR'AN 2:152

It is ALLAH who guides whoever HE WILLS

PERHAPS YOU DISLIKE SOMETHING
WHICH IS GOOD FOR YOU
AND LIKE SOMETHING
WHICH IS BAD FOR YOU.
ALLAH KNOWS, WHILE
YOU KNOW NOT

QUR'AN 2:216

WHOEVER
RELIES UPON ALLAH,
THEN HE IS SUFFICIENT FOR HIM
QUR'AN 65:3

I PRAY...

...THAT THE PEACE YOU SEEK
FINDS ITS WAY TO YOU

My Lord,
I am in need of
whatever good You send
Down to me

QUR'AN 28:24

YOU MIGHT AIM TO
REACH THE STARS,

BUT ALLAH MIGHT HAVE
THE MOON WRITTEN
FOR YOU

SEEK HELP THROUGH PATIENCE AND PRAYER

QUR'AN 2:45

MY LORD,
PUT MY HEART
AT EASE FOR ME

AND EASE MY
TASK FOR ME

QUR'AN 20:25

HE WILL
SOOTHE THE HEARTS
OF THOSE WHO
BELIEVE
QUR'AN 9:14

HE IS WITH YOU
WHEREVER
YOU ARE

QUR'AN 51:4

OH ALLAH,
BRING ME CLOSER
TO YOU

EVery step you take,
May ALLAH
be with you

FIND ALLAH,
AND HAPPINESS WILL FIND YOU

He knows

what lies in...

...EVERY HEART

QUR'AN 67:13

IF THE HURT COMES, SO WILL THE HAPPINESS

QUR'AN 94:5

INDEED, WHAT IS TO COME WILL BE BETTER THAN

WHAT IS GONE BY

QUR'AN 93:4

IN EVERY
DELAY,
THERE IS
GOODNESS

THERE is NOT A LEAF THAT FALLS BUT HE KNOWS IT

QUR'AN 6:59

IN HIM
I PLACE MY
TRUST

QUR'AN 13:30

HE KNOWS WHAT IS IN EVERY HEART

QUR'AN 67:13

VERILY, IN THE REMEMBRANCE OF ALLAH...

...do Hearts find REST

QUR'AN 13:28

SEEK ALLAH IN YOUR
MOMENTS OF BLISS

AND IN YOUR
MOMENTS OF GRIEF

WITH EVERY
HARDSHIP COMES
EASE...
QUR'AN 94:5

HE BRINGS THEM
OUT OF DARKNESS
INTO LIGHT
QUR'AN 2:251

TRULY, TO ALLAH WE **BELON**G AND TRULY, TO HIM WE SHALL RETURN

QUR'AN 2:156

BUT THEY PLAN,
AND ALLAH PLANS

AND ALLAH IS THE
BEST OF PLANNERS

QUR'AN 8:30

OH ALLAH,
RENEW THE IMAN
IN MY HEART

INDEED, ALLAH IS WITH THE PATIENT

QUR'AN 2:153

...THOSE WHO SUFFER
IN SILENCE

ALLAH HAS A
BEAUTIFUL PLAN
FOR YOU

WHATEVER OF BLESSINGS YOU HAVE,

IT IS FROM ALLAH

QUR'AN 16:53

DO NOT LOSE HOPE
NOR BE SAD

QUR'AN 3:139

IN MOMENTS OF
HEAVINESS,
LET PRAYER BE YOUR
COMFORT

MY SUCCESS CAN ONLY COME FROM ALLAH

QUR'AN 11:88

First published by Ebury Press in 2024, an imprint of Ebury Publishing. Ebury Publishing is part of the Penguin Random House group of companies.

Andrews McMeel Publishing
a division of Andrews McMeel Universal
1130 Walnut Street, Kansas City, Missouri 64106
www.andrewsmcmeel.com

25 26 27 28 29 TEN 10 9 8 7 6 5 4 3 2 1

ISBN: 978-1-5248-9790-1

Library of Congress Control Number: 2024946911

Editor: Jean Z. Lucas
Design: maru studio G.K.
Art Director: Julie Barnes
Production Editor: Jennifer Straub
Production Manager: Jeff Preuss

ATTENTION: SCHOOLS AND BUSINESSES
Andrews McMeel books are available at quantity discounts with bulk purchase for educational, business, or sales promotional use. For information, please e-mail the Andrews McMeel Publishing Special Sales Department: sales@andrewsmcmeel.com.